SELENA

DIDN'T

KNOW

SPANISH

EITHER

WINNER OF THE 2021

ROBERT PHILLIPS CHAPBOOK PRIZE

SELECTED BY BENJAMIN GARCIA

Established in 2001, The Robert Phillips Poetry Chapbook Prize highlights one book per year that excels in the chapbook format.

RECENT WINNERS:

Marisa Tirado, *Selena Didn't Know Spanish Either*

Elizabeth Murawski, *Still Life with Timex*

Thomas Nguyen, *Permutations of a Self*

Gregory Byrd, *The Name for the God Who Speaks*

Evana Bodiker, *Ephemera*

FOR THE FULL LIST OF PAST WINNERS SEE:
texasreviewpress.org

SELENA DIDN'T KNOW SPANISH EITHER

POEMS

MARISA TIRADO

THE UNIVERSITY PRESS OF SHSU

For my parents and
my primos

di·as·po·ra

is silent. Is spiritual.
It is being robbed of memoir
while you sleep in a suburb.
It is nonconsensually sensual,
embodying unremarkable
unless enticing, exotic.
It is a study-abroad bilingual
with a job before the nativa,
the hoop earrings disallowed
until anthropologie sells them.
It is considering all the forms
of death around you. A challenge,
an invitation to triumph,
it is Selena Quintanilla
lifting her language
despite all its baggage
and taking it to the Grammys.
It is a question: When it comes for you,
what remnants will you recover?
What will you do to reclaim
all that was forced lost?

CONTENTS

YOUNG MEMOIR

I was born. My ears were christened
with a sewing needle in the kitchen
by my grandmother. White sidewalks warned us
that bilingual kids make playgrounds hostile.
So I sold shortbreads with Girl Scouts
as I climbed the marble ranks. Life broke
more rules, I canoed 52 miles forward
to a sun setting behind me. I saw a tree
rip off the earth and get flicked across the yard
like a scab. I moved west, became a minister.
I flunked the purity exam, was stabbed
by a diamond before it could snail down my finger.
I got stuck in my hair, I fell out
in nine clumps. As we all learn eventually,
everything shatters upwards. Saying yes
is just saying no to a thousand other things.
I searched for it, jogged through the woods,
but healing is not linear. I zig-zagged past the creek,
pulled a piece of glass from my heel
the size of the Narrows Bridge. I found myself
in Hong Kong at a goldfish market, bobbing dumbly
in a plastic bag. Somebody worth forgetting
told me something worth remembering:
There are few things you'll do now
that will fuck up your life when you're 40.
I went to Santa Fe and let the sun in,
unfolding each year per heat. Like you,
I'm on the run. I hiked Mt. Rainier alone on my birthday.
I've never breathed better. The light I see now
startled every one of my Polaroids.

SOARING ABOVE MARQUEZ LIVESTOCK

In seat B23 I tuck my legs like a calf
fresh with life. The window tilts me,

frames sagebrush dotting Rockies,
whose spotted desert hide colors

outside stories and state lines.
This morning I watched an old

proprietor of one third my name
hum like a well-oiled machine

and straighten an old fence between
the bulls and bessies with a swift kick.

"We didn't cross the border, the border
crossed us," she said, spitting to soil

owned for a dozen decades, soil and sun
my cousin spent two days getting dark in

before getting kicked out of the bookstore
for it, *A Tale of Two Cities* snatched

from his amber hands. This is why
my parents sat at our oak table one night,

young and skittish in their skin, mulling
over my second language. I still blush

when I can't roll my tongue along the top
of my teeth to pronounce my own name.

When I sleep, I become a hot air balloon
from the Fiesta every fall, Albuquerque's sky

birthing a colorful herd, hooves pressing old
stories into our foundation, stories now 10,000

feet away, but once close enough to drift into
each night as soon as the moon would blink.

MOM VS. THE CHOLAS

I first picture the concave fence,
her body warping wire, red nails
pushing her face so deep into metal,
a cheek pressed through a pentagon.
I always assume she was wearing one
of her two outfits. But before I get into
how her third didn't come until years later
in a town a thousand miles away,

I want to focus on the fence.
And its crescent bend as six fists
beat my mom into the Española Circle of Life,
their hoops gleaming like lowriders.
But on this day after a seismic bounce
against the chain links, Margie Marquez ducked
and rolled, stood and clouded three cholas[1]
in roadrunner dust. She ran faster than the time

Rob haloed a lasso to her throat, faster
than the rocks Joe pegged with the end
of a piñon root. She had enough fists in her life
to know that when you're chased down Pueblo Street
by cholas, when you got three beautiful but
angry motherfuckers clawing at the wisps of your hair
screamin' *"Next time you kiss Tony Martinez,"*
you take the back route and deal

Cho·la:

a young woman belonging to a Mexican American urban subculture associated with street gangs;
a gorgeous and often misunderstood warrior; desert guardian; man-protector; lowrider shepherd, lord of
the liner; hoop mysticism; bad rap for what; padrina of the tougher side of my blood.

with the horse manure. You climb the dirty hill,
tumble down desert weeds and flatten yourself
against the family feed store. You just run
till you hit something more dangerous.
100 outfits, 1,000 miles, and 100,000 days later,
my mother learned Flamenco.
She never bothered to tell us, just arrived one day
on stage in the spotlight, and we watched. We,

who were never chased by cholas, never saw
a screaming Puerto Rican run her boyfriend over
with a pickup at a party. We, suburban, callow,
wouldn't know to honk the horn inside a car
to escape a knife. No, I've never even had to
mop up my own blood. Never after never
realized, watching her in her light, saved
and saved and saved by her duende.

COMO LA FLOR

Anna Maria, turquoised and pewtered,
dripping with the sky's approval,
aware as a saguaro that it takes
almost fifty years to grow a flower.
Bridesmaids unwither, immune to dirt;
kick leaves off their pumps. Wind reforms
roses around the altar. Today is unconditional,
bouquets conquer tumbleweed. It's as if
her mother is here, not miles away
under another sun. Or as if her brother
could walk her down without crutches,
like his horse never bucked him broken
below the wild moon, *ay cómo le duele,*
bleeding like a blooming yucca.

BEFORE THE REVOLT

After Natalie Diaz

I am on a date. I am asked where my skin came from.
A hundred years ago, a Spaniard stole a matriarch

and put her in his redbrick home. This, I say,
made my skin. Closing his menu, he considers me,

says my culture is trendy. Our food is served
and I envision the woman watching her captor sleep,

kachinas guiding her knife to rib, his red colony spilling
in Santa Fe moonlight. Before the Pueblo Revolt,

leaders untied one knot from a cord at each daybreak.
When the last was untied, it released the attack.

Later while brushing my teeth, I feel these things
slog over, rising in the shower, scalding me

with coping particles. I wash my land
with a bar of soap so small, the hand cannot

fully grasp it. In the fogged mirror I draw a trail
from my ancient self to the self-absorbed face.

The obsession with story is a jarring one,
and the anti-time mask clings to my nose,

clay settling into another layer. If the grief works,
it will mix with steam, open pores, beckon out sediment.

HOW TO MAKE AN ADOBE BRICK

Too much clay
results in shrinking.
It will crack
unless it warps.
Too much sand creates
breakage, tendency to erode,
quickly, after the first
desert rain. Adobe can
only be evaluated
by its strength.
This is not a metaphor.
Can it keep out coyotes?
Will it hold off the militia?
Avoid making adobe
when your heart is weak
or when blood needs spilling,
the bricks will not need
paint, our sun stains it.
Refrain from soils containing
alkali, gypsum, stones
from another's rock garden.
Use tin-lined, strong-willed,
seen-some-shit,

heavy-duty molds.
The light will moderate.
Straw cut very short
will create aesthetically pleasing
adobe, especially when combined
with certain pale colors
and micaceous material.
Like plaster. Like closure.
How many times have you watched
your foundation crack?
Are your hands filthy enough?
Perhaps you notice your brick's
air pockets, but continue
to lay them as heat pops
a blister on your neck.
Your brick must always be
10 x 4 x 14 inches, parallel,
perfect, given peep holes
here or there, a weed
moling toward light
with ambition.

LORENA BOBBITT

O what's in a name?
Three months before I was born
ten policemen stepped gingerly,
held their flashlights and crotches
and searched a gravel field
for John Wayne's dick.
She released it at night
as one does an apple core,
slowed for a hurl from the driver's side
before a swerve back to inertia.
When they found it,
not arm nor any other part,
it was placed on ice
in a hotdog box from the 7-11.
She worked at a nail salon,
sometimes slept in a car.
During the day, she pushed metal plows
down cuticles, harvested nail beds
and their futures,
the myth of more polished,
attached. When I was pulled apart
from my mother's body
she named me Lorena.
I didn't know until I was twenty,
her name crossed out on my papers,

canceled by 90's headlines.
The news and its astrology led to
public shame at a De Los Muertos
fest in Chicago, her name phaunting my mother
as she introduced her baby gnawing
on a sugar skull. O,
be some other name! Lorena,
not yet deemed rape victim,
nor feminist, immigrant icon.
Soon-to-be mental health hero,
budding, tricky sex politician.
Future president's dinner guest.
I once dreamed I met her,
at the beauty shop.
She gave me a manicure,
pink. That which we call a rose
doubted any word would smell as sweet.

EL CHICO DEL APARTAMENTO CINCO DOCE

Camila leaves Santa Fe, rides a horse to Cornell.
Life multiplies, so do her degrees.
Her husband, with POISON tattooed across
his throat, enters. His temperature resists
her heat, unmoved by her warmth. *Pero hoy,*
por fin, ha decidido. She flees their cold flat
on the back of an ancient coyote. She rejoins
her piñon, the old desert embraces its child.
She transforms into a teacher. Students learn
to meditate for the first time, swap Keats with
Anaya for the first time. The sun basks
her adobe apartment, her cowhide couch.
The wind within her still whispers,
the roadrunner stays awake.

LEAVE THIS PLACE

and tell others what a road swallowed
by evergreen can do for darkness.

The burn-marked palm can still feel summer wind,
a thousand benedictions breeze unconditionally.

Looking toward mountain caps I cannot find
what erodes the future into smooth stone. All I crave

is the fullness from a canoe, the exhale
from shore, to row memory, churning it thick,

something mighty to hold everything brought
from myself, upon myself, through myself,

and to spread it over this lake in a thin layer—
which seen with the right eyes, will evaporate,

—making me part of its body, sacred sapphire,
blue sail skin, rippled and pure by moonlight.

JALISCO, MX

México and America clash in my blood and this strip mall, in the lonches steaming in a car trunk and the neon fast food buzz behind it. Today home ignited in my cell count, wordless reunion of self with the selves who created us. The strange stench of what was taken. I met a salon girl who said her mother, too, cleans the house to Santana on Sundays. Later a nightclub bouncer hand-selects rich fresas from the line like conchas for his sugar-dusted tray. I hated myself for acting like a tourist and swallowing a scorpion drowned in alcohol, the expat version of the country's true worm. Tequila soaked, the morning greets me with an ancient dog perched on a rooftop.

TEQUILA, MX

And on the third day, Martín snuck us into a mezcal factory. Agaves thundered out of trucks from the gods. We, mortal, assimilated, tripped over the ancient gourds, escaped by motorbike. Windows opened as we passed in the dust. He laughed like my rascal cousin, waved to his old tía. In search of an ATM, we passed a mural, which showed how the town was struck by lightning years ago. The gods blasted agave, fermented the starry fruit by storm. Legend and fact say, the Spaniards came to steal it. To hinder troops, an Aztec shmoozer visited an enemy camp, threw a party. The generals got so drunk they were tied to a tree, lost their guns. We ride past another tourist trap. Bottle keychain. Aimless dollar. Dim distillery. Martín fights with a bartender who is also his best friend's sister. I don't even like the stuff, she says, pouring another double.

YOUNG MEMOIR

A newborn makes noises that match its sonic culture: ñ's and acoos or English spit bubbles. This is how I felt in the desert streets: ridiculous, fetal, and pre-immersed. I know these sounds, these curls and those eyebrows. I am home, yet confusing every waitress with my strained r's. I see a family straight out of my mother's childhood, laying on a mattress in the back of a pickup. I want to swing from my Uber, ask them who I am. Giant succulents dot the cliffs with a starry shower. A hot moon cooperates with banda blasting, radiating the night till every ocelot retires. Come morning, I push my thumb to a four-wheeler up a highway, droning toward adrenaline, affirming my search with all the empty space ahead.

SPACESUITS

It's more difficult for people like me
to sleep during a full moon;
astronomers are recently concerned
with connections between the white sphere's
distance to my world
and its effect on the tides
in my dreams. Yes, this is stressful,
asking one to comprehend the pull of its gravity
on a planet they will never walk on.
I still see most well-meaning moons as: a moon,
spending its existence orbiting me
to stimulate its power or sympathy.
Sympathy masks many, pandemically,
spiritually. Survive by shrink-wrapping our brains
to accept a father dying alone in a trailer
spray-painted into a hospital room.
To ignore a child, caged under another moon
who makes its way through daytime sky,
acting for today as: a sun.
Spacesuits at the border.
Spacesuits at the airport,
ceremonial spritz of sterile grapefruit.
Once while I trusted a moon with my sleep,

my father bit a sandwich to find inside
a well-meaning bee,
stunned and buzzing about
a world beyond its own.
Then I saw the swarm
escape our porch, taking
traces of our galaxy,
bits of stars at a time.
I looked closer,
saw his shoulder heaves—laughter
—routine digest of simple stingers
down to join the accumulation
from decades past.

CHARLOTTESVILLE, PARKLAND HIGH, ETC. ETC. ETC.

Charlottesville held an altar call,
sorry, said the clergy.
We're not really like this
said the college town,
the crying girl,
the blinking phone.
A few months later
Emma Gonzales let six minutes
and twenty seconds
reverberate from the halls
to the crowds,
marching for lives
after running for them.
rapid fire clicks inform me
on a screen. I lit a candle
to prove daylight surrounds it.
Lit one for the students,
Heather Heyer too.
For the sour-moraled, truth-confused.
Lit some to cancel the ones they used.
No wonder, this urge to avoid.
To unfeel a Dodge Challenger
plowing you from a crowd
and flipping you into air
on the news.

ANCESTRY

Born: my fear of wind
after the microburst's lift
of our two-story fir. I smear
eucalyptus on my shoulders
at night when gales visit and
assimilate every garden stone
from its native self, eroding
my neighborhood to noise.
A basket on our porch
is filled with stones
gathered by my mother,
who once collected some
Gold Butte into her purse
behind a ranger, hacked a lump
from Mt. Rushmore
and stuffed it into my satchel.
She greeted Crazy Horse,
who never conceded,
and allowed herself
a small helping of granite.
This, heavy in my sweatshirt,
reminded that my ancestors
were not white, corrosion
of the sand mirror,
my mother's father limping
toward us through spinning dust,
waving his thirty dollars
refunded per Native Discount.

BIDI BIDI BOM BOM

Celina beats a sun-crusted saddle
with an old broom, a week's worth
of prairie meditations clouding her.
This is the day Alcario fell in love, driving
to her ranch unannounced. Emociona,
ya no razona. As he sets like the Manassa sun
over the front porch, her feet firm
in the mountain dust. She clutches her broom,
hardens her cinnamon face, leaves her hair
as is: a fortified crow's nest, keeps on her apron:
ancient green. Let sweat and dirt
mix with light. Bewitched a heart wave,
he gazes at all that chicken blood
covering those perfect hands.

SELENA DIDN'T KNOW SPANISH EITHER

I could have been bilingual,

missed my father's sonic trust fund.

You see, a local pedagogy said a brain twice as cultural

makes a learning disability. Decades later

and my language is still chalked, sometimes it suffocates me

like when I can hardly speak to my matriarchs, but when I'm sad

I play my favorite song because I have hunger,

I have twenty-eight years, I have Aztec blood

and *Bidibidibidibidibidibidibombom* grounds me

in its chaotic trills and hip-induction.

When I learned that at first, Selena didn't know Spanish either,

I entered a moment beyond my own poetics.

Truth is, white kids get more gold stars per language,

get corporate jobs in Mexico City. I watched them take

family cruises down to meet my ancestors before I could.

Do you know what it's like to be off-limits from yourself?

Bubbling under me has been some ugly, but now I'm thinking

gorgeous lava. Nowadays anger is my new prima, she is loca,

she is perfect and knows what's up. She breaks things

to put them back right. I use a *Learn Spanish*

Through Reaggaton app, my first new words are ruptura

and callaita, but I'll pick it up as fast as my 14-year-old grandpa

in a steel mill. Selena made Tejano cool in Japan. She was scheduled

to tour the world before she was not safe when she thought

she was safe. Sometimes I think that if Selena

was white like Madonna, she might still be alive.

I wonder if people think about that.

I pray her last words were in Spanish, colorful embroidery

unraveling from her. Each ancient sentence

a burst into the light, *cada vez cada vez cada vez.*

YOUNG MEMOIR

When I summon remembrance, go to its glass fiber layer,
found post-pry bar within board and batten, I find the past—

—dried thick and cerulean, hardened in its own bucket.
I learned that to complain at all is to complain of a lack

of things to search for. The formula for youth. The Turquoise-
Browed Motmot from Cozumel, chirping sad recounts

on a Morning Glory branch, retrospecting its parents' migration
to the bleached Swiss Alps. Once I unbuild, sigh, unbuild again,

seek sadness in the woodpile, accept both real and unreal
as ungalvanized and rusted, I can sand the juniper floorboards

of my future, constructed somewhere in Taos. An amber desert son,
a daughter horsing towards me. The more I cry love, the farther she rides past.

THE LAST GOOD WEEK

When the days ferment, stars start self-defining
which life its gas collapsed into. Moments take their temperature

in the story of how things burned. The tale changes yearly,
causation always tilting in correlation between a woman bleaching cow skulls

in a bathtub and the Ford which struck her brother so hard
he became schizophrenic. The skulls sold for forty bucks, enough to take

all the youngest to see *Dirty Dancing* at the Dream Catcher. Perhaps from his
head crater on Calle Chavez, her brother watched his mind life

pass into Española's violet sky, blood murmuring out the left ear.
Eight flanneled kids cooped in a dark theater, watching a glowing body

boosted by strong arms, back arched in eternity, chin cocked to hot light,
as he was was thrown into a stretcher and driven all the way to Monday.

GAINING TRACTION

A year spent swimming in my language
and I find anger everywhere.
My vowels conjugate with trauma.
Adverbs find ancestral fists.
Cuando mis labios se abren
correctamente, el fuego
dentro de mí crece.
Or is it justo?
verdadero?
What would my grandfather
have yelled towards
his Puerto Rican sun?
As I bend deeper
towards the well of it all,
a bilingual teen warns of
my impending reduction,
turning from "gifted"
to glossed over italics.

THE SOURCE HAS EXHAUSTED ITSELF

And so have I. The language became cactus, the tumbleweed changed
the locks. If a painted cattle skull achieved 200 pesos post-death,

how dare I go about 2 o'clock and 4, calling 3 ephemeral before effort?
Consider the scorpion. It can survive in the boiling desert.

It responds to carnal agony like others in artistic agony:
the receptors are in the sizzle-hiss. The behavior is in the situation.

The scorpion flees sunset, hoping its cool hole is that of an antelope squirrel
or an armadillo den, and not a lethal ridge-nosed rattlesnake, who quivers

in its mesa, also worried of extinction. If all were thrown
to the campfire, will mortality be measured by each diligence

to climb out? Or do all burn, watching the brink of themselves
turn ash—a scorpion can hardly make it in even today's Southwest.

But who's to say. The timer goes off, the scorpion has stung, everyone is dinner,
and all else dries into freckles of gypsum, or as they call it, sand.

ALICANTE, SPAIN

My new job is inside a school inside the country
where my ancestors are from, ancestors who pillaged
my other ancestors while they made my blood.

Awkward family reunion. Evil greatest grandfather
from the Cantabrian Mountains, father of fathers
who fought my matriarchs with a swift surname. The fight

is a long one, and today is only its pregnant self.
Moments bless me with language lessons.
Give me a glue stick. Your hair is long. Before I left Chicago,

my student grimaced at my lack of our language
as I sliced the bridge between us with my broken verbs.
While I feel out my vowels in the mercado I am careful

to not retain the European lisp, to preserve the wide
and sweet gulf heard in my grandmother's home.
This is the first conversation of many. That exchange

with the bank teller was only its embarrassing self.
With each learned preposition, the color in my cheeks
return like the red ponds on an eager mango.

Acknowledgments

Variations of these poems first appeared in *Michigan Quarterly Review, Triquarterly, Southern Humanities Review, Denver Quarterly, The Santa Fe Writers' Project, Nowhere Magazine,* and *Sugar House Review.*